Content

Fasting in Quran Surah 2:183

يَـٰٓأَيُّهَا ٱلَّذِينَ ءَامَنُواْ كُتِبَ عَلَيْكُمُ ٱلصِّيَامُ كَمَا كُتِبَ عَلَى ٱلَّذِينَ مِن قَبْلِكُمْ لَعَلَّكُمْ تَتَّقُونَ

O you who have believed, decreed upon you is fasting as it was decreed upon those before you that you may become righteous

Ramadan in Quran Surah 2:185

شَهْرُ رَمَضَانَ ٱلَّذِىٓ أُنزِلَ فِيهِ ٱلْقُرْءَانُ هُدًى لِّلنَّاسِ وَبَيِّنَـٰتٍ مِّنَ ٱلْهُدَىٰ وَٱلْفُرْقَانِ ۚ فَمَن شَهِدَ مِنكُمُ ٱلشَّهْرَ فَلْيَصُمْهُ ۖ وَمَن كَانَ مَرِيضًا أَوْ عَلَىٰ سَفَرٍ فَعِدَّةٌ مِّنْ أَيَّامٍ أُخَرَ ۗ يُرِيدُ ٱللَّهُ بِكُمُ ٱلْيُسْرَ وَلَا يُرِيدُ بِكُمُ ٱلْعُسْرَ وَلِتُكْمِلُواْ ٱلْعِدَّةَ وَلِتُكَبِّرُواْ ٱللَّهَ عَلَىٰ مَا هَدَىٰكُمْ وَلَعَلَّكُمْ تَشْكُرُونَ

The month of Ramadan [is that] in which was revealed the Qur'an, a guidance for the people and clear proofs of guidance and criterion. So whoever sights [the crescent of] the month, let him fast it; and whoever is ill or on a journey - then an equal number of other days. Allah intends for you ease and does not intend for you hardship and [wants] for you to complete the period and to glorify Allah for that [to] which He has guided you; and perhaps you will be grateful

Laylatul-Qadr in Quran Surah 97:1-5

إِنَّآ أَنزَلْنَـٰهُ فِى لَيْلَةِ ٱلْقَدْرِ ۝ وَمَآ أَدْرَىٰكَ مَا لَيْلَةُ ٱلْقَدْرِ ۝ لَيْلَةُ ٱلْقَدْرِ خَيْرٌ مِّنْ أَلْفِ شَهْرٍ ۝ تَنَزَّلُ ٱلْمَلَـٰٓئِكَةُ وَٱلرُّوحُ فِيهَا بِإِذْنِ رَبِّهِم مِّن كُلِّ أَمْرٍ ۝ سَلَـٰمٌ هِىَ حَتَّىٰ مَطْلَعِ ٱلْفَجْرِ ۝

Indeed, We sent it [i.e., the Qur'an] down during the Night of Decree. And what can make you know what is the Night of Decree The Night of Decree is better than a thousand months. The angels and the Spirit [i.e., Gabriel] descend therein by permission of their Lord for every matter. Peace it is until the emergence of dawn

User Guide

This 'Ramadan Planner & Tracking Journal' is developed after extensive research. Using this journal, you can **Plan & Track**, every activity during Ramadan i.e. **Fasting, Quran, Salat, Dhikr, Zakat Charity, Dua, Removal of Bad Habits, Thanking, Saying Sorry, Forgiving, Meals, Work, Sleep, Family, Workout, Weight, Study, Meetings, Visits, Shopping, Gifts, Financials etc**.

Use our simple strategy **'Plan Tomorrow, Track Today'** (figure given bellow), which will help you to get 100% success in your Ramadan Plans, making your Ramadan, one of the best ever, Insha Allah.

In this strategy, you 'Plan Tomorrow' i.e. you plan the Day of 2nd Ramadan, on the 1st Ramadan itself. Different sections in this journal will help you to plan your Ramadan Day with every detail, very easily.

Review your earlier planned activities throughout the day. 'Track Today' i.e. before going to bed every Ramadan Night, track & tick all your earlier planned activities, you completed Today. Self assess yourself & give marking at the end, which will challenge you to be better tomorrow, keeping you energized throughout the Ramadan.

Scan QR Codes given in this journal, by your mobile camera or mobile QR code scanner app & you can directly open the relevant Quran Juz & Islamic Lectures on your mobile cell phone, for that day. **30 Quran Juzs, different 30 Islamic Lectures** for all 30 Days of Ramadan. Scan QR codes given in notes section, at the end of this journal, to see **Live Kaaba Haram Sharif Mecca & Masjid-e-Nabvi Medina**. Scan QR code in notes section, select your nearest major city & country, to get the **Ramadan Fasting Suhoor (Imsak), Iftar & Prayer Times** in your area.

Kindly check **Zakat** pages in end sections, to plan your Zakat.

Learn **30 Names of Allah** & its Meanings. Collect your Ramadan Memories at end & much more !

For help & feedback, kindly contact at www.DeeneeShop.com

May Allah bless you with all the Benefits of Ramadan
As-Salaam-Alaikum (Peace be unto you)

| PLAN .... Tomorrow |
| TRACK Today ✓ |

Ramadan Monthly Ibadah Planner

English Months : _____   Year : _____

MON	TUE	WED	THU	FRI	SAT	SUN

Notes :

....
....
....
....
....
....

To do list :

◯ _____
◯ _____
◯ _____
◯ _____
◯ _____
◯ _____
◯ _____

Ramadan Monthly Work Planner

English Months : _____ Year : _____

MON	TUE	WED	THU	FRI	SAT	SUN

Notes :

....
....
....
....
....
....

To do list :

_____
_____
_____
_____
_____
_____

FASTED

1 Ramadan

Juz' 1 : Al-Fatihah (1:1) - Al-Baqarah (2:141)

A Name of My Allah

AR-RAHMAAN

The Most or Entirely Merciful

My Quran Today	Surah / Ayah	From	To
Arabic Reading	....	....	....
Translation	....	....	....
Memorising	....	....	....
Tafseer	....	....	....

Scan For Today's Quran

My Prayers Today ☑

- Maghrib
- Isha
- Taraweeh
- Tahajjud
- Fajr
- Zuhr
- Asr

My Dhikr Today

- First Kalima e Tayyab ....
- Astaghfaar & Towbah ....
- Alhamdulillah ....
- ....
- ....
- ....
- ....

My Charity Today

- Zakaat ....
- Sadqa ....
- Khairaat ....
- Fitr ....
- Feed Hungry Person ....
- Help Needy Person ....
- ....

My One Bad Habit To Remove Today

Bad Habit : ....

....

Action To Remove It : ....

....

....

....

My Meals Planner

Suhoor : Dates, Water, Honey,

Habbatussauda (Kalonji) ....

....

Iftar : Dates, Water, ...

....

....

Scan For Today's Lecture

Success Strategy

| PLAN .... Tomorrow |
| TRACK Today ✓ |

To be a Better Person, Today, I,

Said **SORRY** to, ..., for ....

Said **THANK YOU** to, ..., for ....

Have **FORGIVEN** to, ..., & I am feeling ....

Phoned / Talked to my **Family Member / Relative / Friend / Neighbour**, ...

Thank Allah for,	Ask Forgiveness from Allah for,	Make Dua to Allah for,
giving you this Ramadan	missed Ibaadah in past Ramadans	Health to Fast & do Ibaadah

English Date : ....

Day : ....

⬤ Any Out Of Town Travel Plan Today : ....

Today's Work Priorities :

⬤ 1...

⬤ 2...

⬤ 3...

⬤ 4...

⬤ 5...

Today's Important Meetings / Calls / Visits :

⬤ 1...

⬤ 2...

⬤ 3...

⬤ 4...

⬤ 5...

Today's Financial / Bills / Payment Priorities :

⬤ 1...

⬤ 2...

⬤ 3...

⬤ 4...

⬤ 5...

Today's Family Priorities :

⬤ 1...

⬤ 2...

⬤ 3...

Today's Shopping List :

⬤ ....   ⬤ ....

⬤ ....   ⬤ ....

⬤ ....   ⬤ ....

⬤ ....   ⬤ ....

My Time Planning Today (in Hours / Minutes)

⬤ Sleep .... ⬤ Work .... ⬤ Ibadaah ....

⬤ Family .... ⬤ Exercise ..... ⬤ Study ....

My Today's Schedule :

2 am
_____
3 am
_____
4 am
_____
5 am
_____
6 am
_____
7 am
_____
8 am
_____
9 am
_____
10 am
_____
11 am
_____
12 noon
_____
1 pm
_____
2 pm
_____
3 pm
_____
4 pm
_____
5 pm
_____
6 pm
_____
7 pm
_____
8 pm
_____
9 pm
_____
10 pm
_____
11 pm
_____
12 midnight
_____
1 am
_____

⬤ **My Weight Today :** ....

Rate Today's Efforts Out of 10 for & Sign

www.DeeneeShop.com

FASTED

2 Ramadan

Juz' 2 : Al-Baqarah (2:142) - Al-Baqarah (2:252)

My Quran Today

	Surah / Ayah	From	To
Arabic Reading	....	....	....
Translation	....	....	....
Memorising	....	....	....
Tafseer	....	....	....

Scan For Today's Quran

My Prayers Today ☑

- Maghrib
- Isha
- Taraweeh
- Tahajjud
- Fajr
- Zuhr
- Asr

My Dhikr Today

- First Kalima e Tayyab ....
- Astaghfaar & Towbah ....
- Alhamdulillah ....
- ....
- ....
- ....
- ....

My Charity Today

- Zakaat ....
- Sadqa ....
- Khairaat ....
- Fitr ....
- Feed Hungry Person ....
- Help Needy Person ....
- ....

My One Bad Habit To Remove Today

- Bad Habit : ....
  ....
- Action To Remove It : ....
  ....
  ....
  ....

My Meals Planner

- Suhoor : Dates, Water, Honey,
  Habbatussauda (Kalonji) ....
  ....
- Iftar : Dates, Water, ...
  ....
  ....

Scan For Today's Lecture

Success Strategy

PLAN Tomorrow	....
TRACK Today	✓

To be a Better Person, Today, I,

- Said **SORRY** to, ..., for ....
- Said **THANK YOU** to, ..., for ....
- Have **FORGIVEN** to, ..., & I am feeling ....
- Phoned / Talked to my **Family Member / Relative / Friend / Neighbour**, ...

Thank Allah for,	**Ask Forgiveness from Allah for,**	**Make Dua to Allah for,**
giving you Islam	mistakes & ignorance in Ibaadah	making you a Better Muslim

English Date : ....

Day : ....

 Any Out Of Town Travel Plan Today : ....

Today's Work Priorities :

 1..

 2..

 3..

 4..

 5..

Today's Important Meetings / Calls / Visits :

 1..

 2..

 3..

 4..

 5..

Today's Financial / Bills / Payment Priorities :

 1..

 2..

 3..

 4..

 5..

Today's Family Priorities :

 1..

 2..

 3..

Today's Shopping List :

 ....

 ....

 ....

 ....

My Time Planning Today (in Hours / Minutes)

 Sleep .... Work .... Ibadaah ....

 Family .... Exercise ..... Study ....

My Today's Schedule :

2 am
----
3 am
----
4 am
----
5 am
----
6 am
----
7 am
----
8 am
----
9 am
----
10 am
----
11 am
----
12 noon
----
1 pm
----
2 pm
----
3 pm
----
4 pm
----
5 pm
----
6 pm
----
7 pm
----
8 pm
----
9 pm
----
10 pm
----
11 pm
----
12 midnight
----
1 am

 My Weight Today : ....

Rate Today's Efforts Out of 10 for & Sign

FASTED

3 Ramadan

Juz' 3 : Al-Baqarah (2:253) - Āli 'Imrân (3:92)

My Quran Today

	Surah / Ayah	From	To
Arabic Reading	....	....	....
Translation	....	....	....
Memorising	....	....	....
Tafseer	....	....	....

Scan For Today's Quran

My Prayers Today ☑

- Maghrib
- Isha
- Taraweeh
- Tahajjud
- Fajr
- Zuhr
- Asr

My Dhikr Today

- First Kalima e Tayyab ....
- Astaghfaar & Towbah ....
- Alhamdulillah ....
- ....
- ....
- ....
- ....

My Charity Today

- Zakaat ....
- Sadqa ....
- Khairaat ....
- Fitr ....
- Feed Hungry Person ....
- Help Needy Person ....

My One Bad Habit To Remove Today

- Bad Habit : ....
  ....
- Action To Remove It : ....
  ....
  ....

My Meals Planner

- Suhoor : Dates, Water, Honey,
  Habbatussauda (Kalonji) ....
  ....
- Iftar : Dates, Water, ...

Scan For Today's Lecture

Success Strategy

PLAN Tomorrow	....
TRACK Today	✓

To be a Better Person, Today, I,

- Said **SORRY** to, ..., for ....
- Said **THANK YOU** to, ..., for ....
- Have **FORGIVEN** to, ..., & I am feeling ....
- Phoned / Talked to my **Family Member / Relative / Friend / Neighbour,** ....

Thank Allah for,	Ask Forgiveness from Allah for,	Make Dua to Allah for,
whatever your Good Health	not caring Allah's given Health to you	People, who are ill

English Date : ....

Day : ....

Any Out Of Town Travel Plan Today : ....

Today's Work Priorities :

1..

2..

3..

4..

5..

Today's Important Meetings / Calls / Visits :

1..

2..

3..

4..

5..

Today's Financial / Bills / Payment Priorities :

1..

2..

3..

4..

5..

Today's Family Priorities :

1..

2..

3..

Today's Shopping List :

....

....

....

....

My Time Planning Today (in Hours / Minutes)

Sleep .... Work .... Ibadaah ....

Family .... Exercise ..... Study ....

My Today's Schedule :

2 am

3 am

4 am

5 am

6 am

7 am

8 am

9 am

10 am

11 am

12 noon

1 pm

2 pm

3 pm

4 pm

5 pm

6 pm

7 pm

8 pm

9 pm

10 pm

11 pm

12 midnight

1 am

My Weight Today : ....

Rate Today's Efforts Out of 10 for & Sign

FASTED

4 Ramadan

Juz' 4 : Āli 'Imrān (3:93) - An-Nisā' (4:23)

My Quran Today

	Surah / Ayah	From	To
Arabic Reading	....	....	....
Translation	....	....	....
Memorising	....	....	....
Tafseer	....	....	....

Scan For Today's Quran

My Prayers Today ☑

- Maghrib
- Isha
- Taraweeh
- Tahajjud
- Fajr
- Zuhr
- Asr

My Dhikr Today

- First Kalima e Tayyab ....
- Astaghfaar & Towbah ....
- Alhamdulillah ....
- ....
- ....
- ....
- ....

My Charity Today

- Zakaat ....
- Sadqa ....
- Khairaat ....
- Fitr ....
- Feed Hungry Person ....
- Help Needy Person ....
- ....

My One Bad Habit To Remove Today

Bad Habit : ....

....

Action To Remove It : ....

....

....

....

My Meals Planner

Suhoor : Dates, Water, Honey,

Habbatussauda (Kalonji) ....

....

Iftar : Dates, Water, ...

....

Scan For Today's Lecture

Success Strategy

PLAN .... Tomorrow
TRACK Today ✓

To be a Better Person, Today, I,

Said **SORRY** to, ..., for ....

Said **THANK YOU** to, ..., for ....

Have **FORGIVEN** to, ..., & I am feeling ....

Phoned / Talked to my **Family Member / Relative / Friend / Neighbour**, ...

Thank Allah for,	**Ask Forgiveness from Allah for,**	**Make Dua to Allah for,**
Food you Eat	Eating Prohibited Food (if any)	People, who don't have Food

English Date : ....

Day : ....

⚬ Any Out Of Town Travel Plan Today : ....

Today's Work Priorities :

⚬ 1...

⚬ 2...

⚬ 3...

⚬ 4...

⚬ 5...

Today's Important Meetings / Calls / Visits :

⚬ 1...

⚬ 2...

⚬ 3...

⚬ 4...

⚬ 5...

Today's Financial / Bills / Payment Priorities :

⚬ 1...

⚬ 2...

⚬ 3...

⚬ 4...

⚬ 5...

Today's Family Priorities :

⚬ 1...

⚬ 2...

⚬ 3...

Today's Shopping List :

⚬ ....   ⚬ ....

⚬ ....   ⚬ ....

⚬ ....   ⚬ ....

⚬ ....   ⚬ ....

My Time Planning Today (in Hours / Minutes)

⚬ Sleep .... ⚬ Work .... ⚬ Ibadaah ....

⚬ Family .... ⚬ Exercise ..... ⚬ Study ....

My Today's Schedule :

2 am
----
3 am
----
4 am
----
5 am
----
6 am
----
7 am
----
8 am
----
9 am
----
10 am
----
11 am
----
12 noon
----
1 pm
----
2 pm
----
3 pm
----
4 pm
----
5 pm
----
6 pm
----
7 pm
----
8 pm
----
9 pm
----
10 pm
----
11 pm
----
12 midnight
----
1 am

⚬ **My Weight Today** : ....

Rate Today's Efforts Out of 10 for & Sign

www.DeeneeShop.com

FASTED

5 Ramadan

Juz' 5 : An-Nisā' (4:24) - An-Nisā' (4:147)

My Quran Today

	Surah / Ayah	From	To
Arabic Reading	....	....	....
Translation	....	....	....
Memorising	....	....	....
Tafseer	....	....	....

Scan For Today's Quran

My Prayers Today ☑

- Maghrib
- Isha
- Taraweeh
- Tahajjud
- Fajr
- Zuhr
- Asr

My Dhikr Today

- First Kalima e Tayyab ....
- Astaghfaar & Towbah ....
- Alhamdulillah ....
- ....
- ....
- ....
- ....

My Charity Today

- Zakaat ....
- Sadqa ....
- Khairaat ....
- Fitr ....
- Feed Hungry Person ....
- Help Needy Person ....
- ....

My One Bad Habit To Remove Today

Bad Habit : ....
....

Action To Remove It : ....
....
....
....

My Meals Planner

Suhoor : Dates, Water, Honey,
Habbatussauda (Kalonji) ....
....
....
Iftar : Dates, Water, ...
....
....

Scan For Today's Lecture

Success
Strategy

PLAN .... Tomorrow
TRACK Today ✓

To be a Better Person, Today, I,

- Said **SORRY** to, ..., for ....
- Said **THANK YOU** to, ..., for ....
- Have **FORGIVEN** to, ..., & I am feeling ....
- Phoned / Talked to my **Family Member / Relative / Friend / Neighbour**, ...

Thank Allah for,	Ask Forgiveness from Allah for,	Make Dua to Allah for,
your Parents (alive or dead)	not serving your Parents, to the full capacity	your Parents

English Date : ....

Day : ....

  Any Out Of Town Travel Plan Today : ....

Today's Work Priorities :

  1...

  2...

  3...

  4...

  5...

Today's Important Meetings / Calls / Visits :

  1...

  2...

  3...

  4...

  5...

Today's Financial / Bills / Payment Priorities :

  1...

  2...

  3...

  4...

  5...

Today's Family Priorities :

  1...

  2...

  3...

Today's Shopping List :

  ....

  ....

  ....

  ....

My Time Planning Today (in Hours / Minutes)

  Sleep ....   Work ....   Ibadaah ....

  Family ....   Exercise .....   Study ....

My Today's Schedule :

2 am
----
3 am
----
4 am
----
5 am
----
6 am
----
7 am
----
8 am
----
9 am
----
10 am
----
11 am
----
12 noon
----
1 pm
----
2 pm
----
3 pm
----
4 pm
----
5 pm
----
6 pm
----
7 pm
----
8 pm
----
9 pm
----
10 pm
----
11 pm
----
12 midnight
----
1 am

  My Weight Today : ....

Rate Today's Efforts Out of 10 for & Sign

FASTED

6 Ramadan

Juz' 6 : An-Nisâ' (4:148) - Al-Mâ'idah (5:82)

My Quran Today

	Surah / Ayah	From	To
Arabic Reading	....	....	....
Translation	....	....	....
Memorising	....	....	....
Tafseer	....	....	....

Scan For Today's Quran

My Prayers Today ☑

- Maghrib
- Isha
- Taraweeh
- Tahajjud
- Fajr
- Zuhr
- Asr

My Dhikr Today

- First Kalima e Tayyab ....
- Astaghfaar & Towbah ....
- Alhamdulillah ....
- ....
- ....
- ....
- ....

My Charity Today

- Zakaat ....
- Sadqa ....
- Khairaat ....
- Fitr ....
- Feed Hungry Person ....
- Help Needy Person ....
- ....

My One Bad Habit To Remove Today

Bad Habit : ....
....
Action To Remove It : ....
....
....
....

My Meals Planner

Suhoor : Dates, Water, Honey,
Habbatussauda (Kalonji) ....
....
Iftar : Dates, Water, ...
....
....

Scan For Today's Lecture

Success Strategy

| PLAN Tomorrow | .... |
| TRACK Today | ✓ |

To be a Better Person, Today, I,

Said **SORRY** to, ..., for ....

Said **THANK YOU** to, ..., for ....

Have **FORGIVEN** to, ..., & I am feeling ....

Phoned / Talked to my **Family Member / Relative / Friend / Neighbour**, ...

Thank Allah for,	Ask Forgiveness from Allah for,	Make Dua to Allah,
your Spouse	not behaving the best, with your Spouse	to get Happiness in each other

English Date : ....

Day : ....

Any Out Of Town Travel Plan Today : ....

Today's Work Priorities :

1...

2...

3...

4...

5...

Today's Important Meetings / Calls / Visits :

1...

2...

3...

4...

5...

Today's Financial / Bills / Payment Priorities :

1...

2...

3...

4...

5...

Today's Family Priorities :

1...

2...

3...

Today's Shopping List :

....

....

....

....

My Time Planning Today (in Hours / Minutes)

Sleep ....   Work ....   Ibadaah ....

Family ....   Exercise .....   Study ....

My Today's Schedule :

2 am
----
3 am
----
4 am
----
5 am
----
6 am
----
7 am
----
8 am
----
9 am
----
10 am
----
11 am
----
12 noon
----
1 pm
----
2 pm
----
3 pm
----
4 pm
----
5 pm
----
6 pm
----
7 pm
----
8 pm
----
9 pm
----
10 pm
----
11 pm
----
12 midnight
----
1 am

My Weight Today : ....

Rate Today's Efforts Out of 10 for & Sign

7 Ramadan

Juz' 7 : Al-Mā'idah (5:83) - Al-An'ām (6:110)

My Quran Today

	Surah / Ayah	From	To
Arabic Reading			
Translation			
Memorising			
Tafseer			

Scan For Today's Quran

My Prayers Today ☑

- Maghrib
- Isha
- Taraweeh
- Tahajjud
- Fajr
- Zuhr
- Asr

My Dhikr Today

- First Kalima e Tayyab ....
- Astaghfaar & Towbah ....
- Alhamdulillah ....
- ....
- ....
- ....
- ....

My Charity Today

- Zakaat ....
- Sadqa ....
- Khairaat ....
- Fitr ....
- Feed Hungry Person ....
- Help Needy Person ....
- ....

My One Bad Habit To Remove Today

Bad Habit : ....
....

Action To Remove It : ....
....
....
....

My Meals Planner

Suhoor : Dates, Water, Honey,
Habbatussauda (Kalonji) ....
....

Iftar : Dates, Water, ...
....
....
....

Scan For Today's Lecture

Success
Strategy

PLAN .... Tomorrow
TRACK Today ✓

To be a Better Person, Today, I,

Said **SORRY** to, ..., for ....

Said **THANK YOU** to, ..., for ....

Have **FORGIVEN** to, ..., & I am feeling ....

Phoned / Talked to my **Family Member / Relative / Friend / Neighbour**, ...

Thank Allah for,	Ask Forgiveness from Allah for,	Make Dua to Allah for,
your Child or Children	not being the best, to your Child or Children	Good Health of your Children

English Date : ....

Day : ....

Any Out Of Town Travel Plan Today : ....

Today's Work Priorities :

1...
2...
3...
4...
5...

Today's Important Meetings / Calls / Visits :

1...
2...
3...
4...
5...

Today's Financial / Bills / Payment Priorities :

1...
2...
3...
4...
5...

Today's Family Priorities :

1...
2...
3...

Today's Shopping List :

....
....
....
....

My Time Planning Today (in Hours / Minutes)

Sleep .... Work .... Ibadaah ....

Family .... Exercise ..... Study ....

My Today's Schedule :

2 am
3 am
4 am
5 am
6 am
7 am
8 am
9 am
10 am
11 am
12 noon
1 pm
2 pm
3 pm
4 pm
5 pm
6 pm
7 pm
8 pm
9 pm
10 pm
11 pm
12 midnight
1 am

My Weight Today : ....

Rate Today's Efforts Out of 10 for & Sign

8 Ramadan

FASTED

Juz' 8 : Al-An'âm (6:111) - Al-A'râf (7:87)

My Quran Today

	Surah / Ayah	From	To
Arabic Reading	....	....	....
Translation	....	....	....
Memorising	....	....	....
Tafseer	....	....	....

Scan For Today's Quran

My Prayers Today ☑

- Maghrib
- Isha
- Taraweeh
- Tahajjud
- Fajr
- Zuhr
- Asr

My Dhikr Today

- First Kalima e Tayyab ....
- Astaghfaar & Towbah ....
- Alhamdulillah ....
- ....
- ....
- ....
- ....

My Charity Today

- Zakaat ....
- Sadqa ....
- Khairaat ....
- Fitr ....
- Feed Hungry Person ....
- Help Needy Person ....
- ....

My One Bad Habit To Remove Today

Bad Habit : ....
....

Action To Remove It : ....
....
....
....

My Meals Planner

Suhoor : Dates, Water, Honey,
Habbatussauda (Kalonji) ....
....
Iftar : Dates, Water, ...
....
....

Scan For Today's Lecture

Success — PLAN .... Tomorrow
Strategy — TRACK Today ✓

To be a Better Person, Today, I,

- Said **SORRY** to, ..., for ....
- Said **THANK YOU** to, ..., for ....
- Have **FORGIVEN** to, ..., & I am feeling ....
- Phoned / Talked to my **Family Member / Relative / Friend / Neighbour**, ...

Thank Allah for,	Ask Forgiveness from Allah for,	Make Dua to Allah for,
your Brothers & Sisters	you not being the Best Brother or Sister	Good Health of your Siblings

English Date : ....

Day : ....

   Any Out Of Town Travel Plan Today : ....

Today's Work Priorities :

   1..

   2..

   3..

   4..

   5..

Today's Important Meetings / Calls / Visits :

   1..

   2..

   3..

   4..

   5..

Today's Financial / Bills / Payment Priorities :

   1..

   2..

   3..

   4..

   5..

Today's Family Priorities :

   1..

   2..

   3..

Today's Shopping List :

   ....

   ....

   ....

   ....

My Time Planning Today (in Hours / Minutes)

   Sleep ....   Work ....   Ibadaah ....

   Family ....   Exercise .....   Study ....

My Today's Schedule :

2 am
_____
3 am
_____
4 am
_____
5 am
_____
6 am
_____
7 am
_____
8 am
_____
9 am
_____
10 am
_____
11 am
_____
12 noon
_____
1 pm
_____
2 pm
_____
3 pm
_____
4 pm
_____
5 pm
_____
6 pm
_____
7 pm
_____
8 pm
_____
9 pm
_____
10 pm
_____
11 pm
_____
12 midnight
_____
1 am
_____

   My Weight Today : ....

Rate Today's Efforts Out of 10 for & Sign

FASTED

9 Ramadan

Juz' 9 : Al-A'rāf (7:88) – Al-Anfāl (8:40)

My Quran Today

	Surah / Ayah	From	To
Arabic Reading	....	....	....
Translation	....	....	....
Memorising	....	....	....
Tafseer	....	....	....

Scan For Today's Quran

My Prayers Today ☑

- Maghrib
- Isha
- Taraweeh
- Tahajjud
- Fajr
- Zuhr
- Asr

My Dhikr Today

- First Kalima e Tayyab ....
- Astaghfaar & Towbah ....
- Alhamdulillah ....
- ....
- ....
- ....
- ....

My Charity Today

- Zakaat ....
- Sadqa ....
- Khairaat ....
- Fitr ....
- Feed Hungry Person ....
- Help Needy Person ....
- ....

My One Bad Habit To Remove Today

Bad Habit : ....

....

Action To Remove It : ....

....

....

....

My Meals Planner

Suhoor : Dates, Water, Honey,

Habbatussauda (Kalonji) ....

....

Iftar : Dates, Water, ...

....

....

Scan For Today's Lecture

Success | PLAN ....
Strategy | Tomorrow
 | TRACK ✓
 | Today

To be a Better Person, Today, I,

Said **SORRY** to, ..., for ....

Said **THANK YOU** to, ..., for ....

Have **FORGIVEN** to, ..., & I am feeling ....

Phoned / Talked to my **Family Member / Relative / Friend / Neighbour,** ....

Thank Allah for,	Ask Forgiveness from Allah for,	Make Dua to Allah for,
your Rizk (Income)	the Haram Rizk you earned (if any)	Only Halal Rizk (Income)

English Date : ....

Day : ....

○ Any Out Of Town Travel Plan Today : ....

Today's Work Priorities :

○ 1..

○ 2..

○ 3..

○ 4..

○ 5..

Today's Important Meetings / Calls / Visits :

○ 1..

○ 2..

○ 3..

○ 4..

○ 5..

Today's Financial / Bills / Payment Priorities :

○ 1..

○ 2..

○ 3..

○ 4..

○ 5..

Today's Family Priorities :

○ 1..

○ 2..

○ 3..

Today's Shopping List :

○ ....   ○ ....

○ ....   ○ ....

○ ....   ○ ....

○ ....   ○ ....

My Time Planning Today (in Hours / Minutes)

○ Sleep ....   ○ Work ....   ○ Ibadaah ....

○ Family ....   ○ Exercise .....   ○ Study ....

My Today's Schedule :

2 am

3 am

4 am

5 am

6 am

7 am

8 am

9 am

10 am

11 am

12 noon

1 pm

2 pm

3 pm

4 pm

5 pm

6 pm

7 pm

8 pm

9 pm

10 pm

11 pm

12 midnight

1 am

○ **My Weight Today :** ....

Rate Today's Efforts Out of 10 for & Sign

FASTED

10 Ramadan
Juz' 10 : Al-Anfâl (8:41) - At-Tawbah (9:92)

A Name of My Allah

AL-MUTAKABBIR
The Supreme, The Majestic

My Quran Today

	Surah / Ayah	From	To
Arabic Reading	....	....	....
Translation	....	....	....
Memorising	....	....	....
Tafseer	....	....	....

Scan For Today's Quran

My Prayers Today ☑

- Maghrib
- Isha
- Taraweeh
- Tahajjud
- Fajr
- Zuhr
- Asr

My Dhikr Today

- First Kalima e Tayyab ....
- Astaghfaar & Towbah ....
- Alhamdulillah ....
- ....
- ....
- ....
- ....

My Charity Today

- Zakaat ....
- Sadqa ....
- Khairaat ....
- Fitr ....
- Feed Hungry Person ....
- Help Needy Person ....
- ....

My One Bad Habit To Remove Today

- Bad Habit : ....
....
- Action To Remove It : ....
....
....
....

My Meals Planner

- Suhoor : Dates, Water, Honey,
Habbatussauda (Kalonji) ....
....
- Iftar : Dates, Water, ...
....
....

Scan For Today's Lecture

Success
Strategy

PLAN .... Tomorrow
TRACK Today ✓

To be a Better Person, Today, I,

- Said **SORRY** to, ..., for ....
- Said **THANK YOU** to, ..., for ....
- Have **FORGIVEN** to, ..., & I am feeling ....
- Phoned / Talked to my **Family Member / Relative / Friend / Neighbour**, ...

Thank Allah for,	Ask Forgiveness from Allah for,	Make Dua to Allah for,
your Home (owned or not)	not making your Home, the best of a Muslim	Peace & Protection in Home

English Date : ....

Day : ....

⬤ Any Out Of Town Travel Plan Today : ....

Today's Work Priorities :

⬤ 1..

⬤ 2..

⬤ 3..

⬤ 4..

⬤ 5..

Today's Important Meetings / Calls / Visits :

⬤ 1..

⬤ 2..

⬤ 3..

⬤ 4..

⬤ 5..

Today's Financial / Bills / Payment Priorities :

⬤ 1..

⬤ 2..

⬤ 3..

⬤ 4..

⬤ 5..

Today's Family Priorities :

⬤ 1..

⬤ 2..

⬤ 3..

Today's Shopping List :

⬤ ....   ⬤ ....

⬤ ....   ⬤ ....

⬤ ....   ⬤ ....

⬤ ....   ⬤ ....

My Time Planning Today (in Hours / Minutes)

⬤ Sleep .... ⬤ Work .... ⬤ Ibadaah ....

⬤ Family .... ⬤ Exercise ..... ⬤ Study ....

My Today's Schedule :

2 am
----
3 am
----
4 am
----
5 am
----
6 am
----
7 am
----
8 am
----
9 am
----
10 am
----
11 am
----
12 noon
----
1 pm
----
2 pm
----
3 pm
----
4 pm
----
5 pm
----
6 pm
----
7 pm
----
8 pm
----
9 pm
----
10 pm
----
11 pm
----
12 midnight
----
1 am

⬤ **My Weight Today :** ....

Rate Today's Efforts Out of 10 for & Sign

FASTED

11 Ramadan

Juz' 11 : At-Tawbah (9:93) - Hūd (11:5)

My Quran Today

	Surah / Ayah	From	To
Arabic Reading	....	......	......
Translation	....	......	......
Memorising	....	......	......
Tafseer	....	......	......

Scan For Today's Quran

My Prayers Today ☑

Maghrib

Isha

Taraweeh

Tahajjud

Fajr

Zuhr

Asr

My Dhikr Today

First Kalima e Tayyab ....

Astaghfaar & Towbah ....

Alhamdulillah ....

....

....

....

....

My Charity Today

Zakaat ....

Sadqa ....

Khairaat ....

Fitr ....

Feed Hungry Person ....

Help Needy Person ....

....

My One Bad Habit To Remove Today

Bad Habit : ....

....

Action To Remove It : ....

....

....

....

My Meals Planner

Suhoor : Dates, Water, Honey,

Habbatussauda (Kalonji) ....

....

Iftar : Dates, Water, ...

....

....

Scan For Today's Lecture

Success Strategy

PLAN	....
Tomorrow	
TRACK	✓
Today	

To be a Better Person, Today, I,

Said **SORRY** to, ..., for ....

Said **THANK YOU** to, ..., for ....

Have **FORGIVEN** to, ..., & I am feeling ....

Phoned / Talked to my **Family Member / Relative / Friend / Neighbour**, ...

Thank Allah for,	Ask Forgiveness from Allah for,	Make Dua to Allah for,
any Free Time you get	not using spare Time for doing Good Deads	Barkaah in Time

English Date : ....

Day : ....

○ Any Out Of Town Travel Plan Today : ....

Today's Work Priorities :

○ 1...

○ 2...

○ 3...

○ 4...

○ 5...

Today's Important Meetings / Calls / Visits :

○ 1...

○ 2...

○ 3...

○ 4...

○ 5...

Today's Financial / Bills / Payment Priorities :

○ 1...

○ 2...

○ 3...

○ 4...

○ 5...

Today's Family Priorities :

○ 1...

○ 2...

○ 3...

Today's Shopping List :

○ ....   ○ ....

○ ....   ○ ....

○ ....   ○ ....

○ ....   ○ ....

My Time Planning Today (in Hours / Minutes)

○ Sleep .... ○ Work .... ○ Ibadaah ....

○ Family .... ○ Exercise ..... ○ Study ....

My Today's Schedule :

2 am
----
3 am
----
4 am
----
5 am
----
6 am
----
7 am
----
8 am
----
9 am
----
10 am
----
11 am
----
12 noon
----
1 pm
----
2 pm
----
3 pm
----
4 pm
----
5 pm
----
6 pm
----
7 pm
----
8 pm
----
9 pm
----
10 pm
----
11 pm
----
12 midnight
----
1 am

○ **My Weight Today** : ....

Rate Today's Efforts Out of 10 for & Sign

12 Ramadan

Juz' 12 : Hūd (11:6) - Yūsuf (12:52)

My Quran Today

	Surah / Ayah	From	To
Arabic Reading	....	....	....
Translation	....	....	....
Memorising	....	....	....
Tafseer	....	....	....

Scan For Today's Quran

My Prayers Today ☑

- Maghrib
- Isha
- Taraweeh
- Tahajjud
- Fajr
- Zuhr
- Asr

My Dhikr Today

- First Kalima e Tayyab ....
- Astaghfaar & Towbah ....
- Alhamdulillah ....
- ....
- ....
- ....
- ....

My Charity Today

- Zakaat ....
- Sadqa ....
- Khairaat ....
- Fitr ....
- Feed Hungry Person ....
- Help Needy Person ....
- ....

My One Bad Habit To Remove Today

Bad Habit : ....

....

Action To Remove It : ....

....

....

....

My Meals Planner

Suhoor : Dates, Water, Honey,

Habbatussauda (Kalonji) ....

....

Iftar : Dates, Water, ...

....

....

Scan For Today's Lecture

Success Strategy

PLAN	....
Tomorrow	
TRACK Today	✓

To be a Better Person, Today, I,

Said **SORRY** to, ..., for ....

Said **THANK YOU** to, ..., for ....

Have **FORGIVEN** to, ..., & I am feeling ....

Phoned / Talked to my **Family Member / Relative / Friend / Neighbour**, ...

Thank Allah for,	Ask Forgiveness from Allah for,	Make Dua to Allah for,
your Eyes, you see from	Seeing Prohibited Things	Heathy Beautiful Eyes

English Date : ....

Day : ....

Any Out Of Town Travel Plan Today : ....

Today's Work Priorities :

1..
2..
3..
4..
5..

Today's Important Meetings / Calls / Visits :

1..
2..
3..
4..
5..

Today's Financial / Bills / Payment Priorities :

1..
2..
3..
4..
5..

Today's Family Priorities :

1..
2..
3..

Today's Shopping List :

....
....
....
....

My Time Planning Today (in Hours / Minutes)

Sleep ....   Work ....   Ibadaah ....

Family ....   Exercise .....   Study ....

My Today's Schedule :

2 am
----
3 am
----
4 am
----
5 am
----
6 am
----
7 am
----
8 am
----
9 am
----
10 am
----
11 am
----
12 noon
----
1 pm
----
2 pm
----
3 pm
----
4 pm
----
5 pm
----
6 pm
----
7 pm
----
8 pm
----
9 pm
----
10 pm
----
11 pm
----
12 midnight
----
1 am

My Weight Today : ....

Rate Today's Efforts Out of 10 for & Sign

FASTED

13 Ramadan

Juz' 13 : Yūsuf (12:53) - Ibrāhīm (14:52)

My Quran Today

	Surah / Ayah	From	To
Arabic Reading	....	....	....
Translation	....	....	....
Memorising	....	....	....
Tafseer	....	....	....

Scan For Today's Quran

My Prayers Today ☑

- Maghrib
- Isha
- Taraweeh
- Tahajjud
- Fajr
- Zuhr
- Asr

My Dhikr Today

- First Kalima e Tayyab ....
- Astaghfaar & Towbah ....
- Alhamdulillah ....
- ....
- ....
- ....
- ....

My Charity Today

- Zakaat ....
- Sadqa ....
- Khairaat ....
- Fitr ....
- Feed Hungry Person ....
- Help Needy Person ....
- ....

My One Bad Habit To Remove Today

Bad Habit : ....

....

Action To Remove It : ....

....

....

....

My Meals Planner

Suhoor : Dates, Water, Honey,

Habbatussauda (Kalonji) ....

....

Iftar : Dates, Water, ...

....

....

Scan For Today's Lecture

Success | PLAN ....
Strategy | Tomorrow
| TRACK ✔
| Today

To be a Better Person, Today, I,

Said **SORRY** to, ..., for ....

Said **THANK YOU** to, ..., for ....

Have **FORGIVEN** to, ..., & I am feeling ....

Phoned / Talked to my **Family Member / Relative / Friend / Neighbour**, ...

Thank Allah for,	Ask Forgiveness from Allah for,	Make Dua to Allah for,
your Ears, you hear from	Hearing Prohibited Things	Focus & Concentration in Salats

English Date : ....

Day : ....

○ Any Out Of Town Travel Plan Today : ....

Today's Work Priorities :

○ 1..

○ 2..

○ 3..

○ 4..

○ 5..

Today's Important Meetings / Calls / Visits :

○ 1..

○ 2..

○ 3..

○ 4..

○ 5..

Today's Financial / Bills / Payment Priorities :

○ 1..

○ 2..

○ 3..

○ 4..

○ 5..

Today's Family Priorities :

○ 1..

○ 2..

○ 3..

Today's Shopping List :

○ ....   ○ ....

○ ....   ○ ....

○ ....   ○ ....

○ ....   ○ ....

My Time Planning Today (in Hours / Minutes)

○ Sleep .... ○ Work .... ○ Ibadaah ....

○ Family .... ○ Exercise ..... ○ Study ....

My Today's Schedule :

2 am
----
3 am
----
4 am
----
5 am
----
6 am
----
7 am
----
8 am
----
9 am
----
10 am
----
11 am
----
12 noon
----
1 pm
----
2 pm
----
3 pm
----
4 pm
----
5 pm
----
6 pm
----
7 pm
----
8 pm
----
9 pm
----
10 pm
----
11 pm
----
12 midnight
----
1 am

○ My Weight Today : ....

Rate Today's Efforts Out of 10 for & Sign

14 Ramadan

Juz' 14 : Al-Hijr (15:1) - An-Naḥl (16:128)

AL-GHAFFAR

The All- and Oft-Forgiving

My Quran Today

	Surah / Ayah	From	To
Arabic Reading	....	....	....
Translation	....	....	....
Memorising	....	....	....
Tafseer	....	....	....

Scan For Today's Quran

My Prayers Today ☑

- Maghrib
- Isha
- Taraweeh
- Tahajjud
- Fajr
- Zuhr
- Asr

My Dhikr Today

- First Kalima e Tayyab ....
- Astaghfaar & Towbah ....
- Alhamdulillah ....
- ....
- ....
- ....
- ....

My Charity Today

- Zakaat ....
- Sadqa ....
- Khairaat ....
- Fitr ....
- Feed Hungry Person ....
- Help Needy Person ....
- ....

My One Bad Habit To Remove Today

Bad Habit : ....

....

Action To Remove It : ....

....

....

....

My Meals Planner

Suhoor : Dates, Water, Honey,

Habbatussauda (Kalonji) ....

....

Iftar : Dates, Water, ...

....

....

Scan For Today's Lecture

Success
Strategy

PLAN ....
Tomorrow
TRACK
Today ✓

To be a Better Person, Today, I,

Said **SORRY** to, ..., for ....

Said **THANK YOU** to, ..., for ....

Have **FORGIVEN** to, ..., & I am feeling ....

Phoned / Talked to my **Family Member / Relative / Friend / Neighbour**, ...

Thank Allah for,	**Ask Forgiveness from Allah for,**	**Make Dua to Allah for,**
your Mouth, you speak & eat	Speaking Bad Things	giviing you Sabr (Patience)

English Date : ....

Day : ....

🌸 Any Out Of Town Travel Plan Today : ....

Today's Work Priorities :

🌸 1...

🌸 2...

🌸 3...

🌸 4...

🌸 5...

Today's Important Meetings / Calls / Visits :

🌸 1...

🌸 2...

🌸 3...

🌸 4...

🌸 5...

Today's Financial / Bills / Payment Priorities :

🌸 1...

🌸 2...

🌸 3...

🌸 4...

🌸 5...

Today's Family Priorities :

🌸 1...

🌸 2...

🌸 3...

Today's Shopping List :

🌸 .... 🌸 ....

🌸 .... 🌸 ....

🌸 .... 🌸 ....

🌸 .... 🌸 ....

My Time Planning Today (in Hours / Minutes)

🌸 Sleep .... 🌸 Work .... 🌸 Ibadaah ....

🌸 Family .... 🌸 Exercise ..... 🌸 Study ....

My Today's Schedule :

2 am
_____
3 am
_____
4 am
_____
5 am
_____
6 am
_____
7 am
_____
8 am
_____
9 am
_____
10 am
_____
11 am
_____
12 noon
_____
1 pm
_____
2 pm
_____
3 pm
_____
4 pm
_____
5 pm
_____
6 pm
_____
7 pm
_____
8 pm
_____
9 pm
_____
10 pm
_____
11 pm
_____
12 midnight
_____
1 am
_____

🌸 **My Weight Today :** ....

Rate Today's Efforts Out of 10 for & Sign

www.DeeneeShop.com

FASTED

15 Ramadan

Juz' 15 : Al-Isrā' (17:1) - Al-Kahf (18:74)

My Quran Today

	Surah / Ayah	From	To
Arabic Reading	....	....	....
Translation	....	....	....
Memorising	....	....	....
Tafseer	....	....	....

Scan For Today's Quran

My Prayers Today ☑

- Maghrib
- Isha
- Taraweeh
- Tahajjud
- Fajr
- Zuhr
- Asr

My Dhikr Today

- First Kalima e Tayyab ....
- Astaghfaar & Towbah ....
- Alhamdulillah ....
- ....
- ....
- ....
- ....

My Charity Today

- Zakaat ....
- Sadqa ....
- Khairaat ....
- Fitr ....
- Feed Hungry Person ....
- Help Needy Person ....
- ....

My One Bad Habit To Remove Today

Bad Habit : ....

....

Action To Remove It : ....

....

....

....

My Meals Planner

Suhoor : Dates, Water, Honey,

Habbatussauda (Kalonji) ....

....

Iftar : Dates, Water, ...

....

....

Scan For Today's Lecture

Success Strategy

PLAN	....
Tomorrow	
TRACK Today	✓

To be a Better Person, Today, I,

Said **SORRY** to, ..., for ....

Said **THANK YOU** to, ..., for ....

Have **FORGIVEN** to, ..., & I am feeling ....

Phoned / Talked to my **Family Member / Relative / Friend / Neighbour**, ...

Thank Allah for,	Ask Forgiveness from Allah for,	Make Dua to Allah for,
your Hands & Legs	Doing Wrong Things with your Hands & Legs	Protection from Accidents

English Date : ....

Day : ....

Any Out Of Town Travel Plan Today : ....

Today's Work Priorities :

1. ....
2. ....
3. ....
4. ....
5. ....

Today's Important Meetings / Calls / Visits :

1. ....
2. ....
3. ....
4. ....
5. ....

Today's Financial / Bills / Payment Priorities :

1. ....
2. ....
3. ....
4. ....
5. ....

Today's Family Priorities :

1. ....
2. ....
3. ....

Today's Shopping List :

....
....
....
....

My Time Planning Today (in Hours / Minutes)

Sleep .... Work .... Ibadaah ....

Family .... Exercise ..... Study ....

My Today's Schedule :

2 am
----
3 am
----
4 am
----
5 am
----
6 am
----
7 am
----
8 am
----
9 am
----
10 am
----
11 am
----
12 noon
----
1 pm
----
2 pm
----
3 pm
----
4 pm
----
5 pm
----
6 pm
----
7 pm
----
8 pm
----
9 pm
----
10 pm
----
11 pm
----
12 midnight
----
1 am

My Weight Today : ....

Rate Today's Efforts Out of 10 for & Sign

FASTED

16 Ramadan

Juz' 16 : Al-Kahf (18:75) - Ṭā Hā (20:135)

My Quran Today

	Surah / Ayah	From	To
Arabic Reading	....	....	....
Translation	....	....	....
Memorising	....	....	....
Tafseer	....	....	....

Scan For Today's Quran

My Prayers Today ☑

- Maghrib
- Isha
- Taraweeh
- Tahajjud
- Fajr
- Zuhr
- Asr

My Dhikr Today

- First Kalima e Tayyab ....
- Astaghfaar & Towbah ....
- Alhamdulillah ....
- ....
- ....
- ....
- ....

My Charity Today

- Zakaat ....
- Sadqa ....
- Khairaat ....
- Fitr ....
- Feed Hungry Person ....
- Help Needy Person ....
- ....

My One Bad Habit To Remove Today

Bad Habit : ....

....

Action To Remove It : ....

....

....

....

My Meals Planner

Suhoor : Dates, Water, Honey,

Habbatussauda (Kalonji) ....

....

Iftar : Dates, Water, ...

....

....

Scan For Today's Lecture

Success | PLAN ....
Strategy Tomorrow

TRACK ✓
Today

To be a Better Person, Today, I,

- Said **SORRY** to, ..., for ....
- Said **THANK YOU** to, ..., for ....
- Have **FORGIVEN** to, ..., & I am feeling ....
- Phoned / Talked to my **Family Member / Relative / Friend / Neighbour**, ...

Thank Allah for,	Ask Forgiveness from Allah for,	Make Dua to Allah for,
whatever Education you have	not using your Education & Skills for Humanity	Kids, who can't afford Education

English Date : ....

Day : ....

Any Out Of Town Travel Plan Today : ....

Today's Work Priorities :

1. ....
2. ....
3. ....
4. ....
5. ....

Today's Important Meetings / Calls / Visits :

1. ....
2. ....
3. ....
4. ....
5. ....

Today's Financial / Bills / Payment Priorities :

1. ....
2. ....
3. ....
4. ....
5. ....

Today's Family Priorities :

1. ....
2. ....
3. ....

Today's Shopping List :

....
....
....
....

My Time Planning Today (in Hours / Minutes)

Sleep .... Work .... Ibadaah ....

Family .... Exercise ..... Study ....

My Today's Schedule :

2 am
----
3 am
----
4 am
----
5 am
----
6 am
----
7 am
----
8 am
----
9 am
----
10 am
----
11 am
----
12 noon
----
1 pm
----
2 pm
----
3 pm
----
4 pm
----
5 pm
----
6 pm
----
7 pm
----
8 pm
----
9 pm
----
10 pm
----
11 pm
----
12 midnight
----
1 am

My Weight Today : ....

Rate Today's Efforts Out of 10 for & Sign

FASTED

17 Ramadan

Juz' 17 : Al-Anbiyā' (21:1) - Al-Ḥajj (22:78)

My Quran Today

	Surah / Ayah	From	To
Arabic Reading	....	....	....
Translation	....	....	....
Memorising	....	....	....
Tafseer	....	....	....

Scan For Today's Quran

My Prayers Today ☑

- Maghrib
- Isha
- Taraweeh
- Tahajjud
- Fajr
- Zuhr
- Asr

My Dhikr Today

- First Kalima e Tayyab ....
- Astaghfaar & Towbah ....
- Alhamdulillah ....
- ....
- ....
- ....
- ....

My Charity Today

- Zakaat ....
- Sadqa ....
- Khairaat ....
- Fitr ....
- Feed Hungry Person ....
- Help Needy Person ....
- ....

My One Bad Habit To Remove Today

Bad Habit : ....
....

Action To Remove It : ....
....
....
....

My Meals Planner

Suhoor : Dates, Water, Honey,
Habbatussauda (Kalonji) ....
....

Iftar : Dates, Water, ...
....
....

Scan For Today's Lecture

Success Strategy

PLAN .... Tomorrow
TRACK Today ✓

To be a Better Person, Today, I,

Said **SORRY** to, ..., for ....

Said **THANK YOU** to, ..., for ....

Have **FORGIVEN** to, ..., & I am feeling ....

Phoned / Talked to my **Family Member / Relative / Friend / Neighbour**, ...

Thank Allah for,	**Ask Forgiveness from Allah for,**	**Make Dua to Allah for,**
giving you Stregth, to Fast	missed Ramadan Fasts, in Past	Rizk (Income) to Feed Poors

English Date : ....

Day : ....

○ Any Out Of Town Travel Plan Today : ....

Today's Work Priorities :

○ 1...

○ 2...

○ 3...

○ 4...

○ 5...

Today's Important Meetings / Calls / Visits :

○ 1...

○ 2...

○ 3...

○ 4...

○ 5...

Today's Financial / Bills / Payment Priorities :

○ 1...

○ 2...

○ 3...

○ 4...

○ 5...

Today's Family Priorities :

○ 1...

○ 2...

○ 3...

Today's Shopping List :

○ ....   ○ ....

○ ....   ○ ....

○ ....   ○ ....

○ ....   ○ ....

My Time Planning Today (in Hours / Minutes)

○ Sleep .... ○ Work .... ○ Ibadaah ....

○ Family .... ○ Exercise ..... ○ Study ....

My Today's Schedule :

2 am

3 am

4 am

5 am

6 am

7 am

8 am

9 am

10 am

11 am

12 noon

1 pm

2 pm

3 pm

4 pm

5 pm

6 pm

7 pm

8 pm

9 pm

10 pm

11 pm

12 midnight

1 am

○ **My Weight Today :** ....

Rate Today's Efforts Out of 10 for & Sign

FASTED

18 Ramadan

Juz' 18 : Al-Mu'minūn (23:1) - Al-Furqān (25:20)

A Name of My Allah

AL-FATTAAH

The Opener, The Judge

My Quran Today

	Surah / Ayah	From	To
Arabic Reading	....	....	....
Translation	....	....	....
Memorising	....	....	....
Tafseer	....	....	....

Scan For Today's Quran

My Prayers Today ☑

- Maghrib
- Isha
- Taraweeh
- Tahajjud
- Fajr
- Zuhr
- Asr

My Dhikr Today

- First Kalima e Tayyab ....
- Astaghfaar & Towbah ....
- Alhamdulillah ....
- ....
- ....
- ....
- ....

My Charity Today

- Zakaat ....
- Sadqa ....
- Khairaat ....
- Fitr ....
- Feed Hungry Person ....
- Help Needy Person ....
- ....

My One Bad Habit To Remove Today

Bad Habit : ....
....

Action To Remove It : ....
....
....
....

My Meals Planner

Suhoor : Dates, Water, Honey, Habbatussauda (Kalonji) ....
....

Iftar : Dates, Water, ...
....
....

Scan For Today's Lecture

Success Strategy

PLAN Tomorrow	....
TRACK Today	✓

To be a Better Person, Today, I,

Said **SORRY** to, ..., for ....

Said **THANK YOU** to, ..., for ....

Have **FORGIVEN** to, ..., & I am feeling ....

Phoned / Talked to my **Family Member / Relative / Friend / Neighbour**, ...

Thank Allah for,	Ask Forgiveness from Allah for,	Make Dua to Allah for,
Sleep	those Prohibited Sleepless Nights (if any)	Comfortable Sleep

English Date : ....

Day : ....

Any Out Of Town Travel Plan Today : ....

Today's Work Priorities :

1..
2..
3..
4..
5..

Today's Important Meetings / Calls / Visits :

1..
2..
3..
4..
5..

Today's Financial / Bills / Payment Priorities :

1..
2..
3..
4..
5..

Today's Family Priorities :

1..
2..
3..

Today's Shopping List :

....
....
....
....

My Time Planning Today (in Hours / Minutes)

Sleep .... Work .... Ibadaah ....

Family .... Exercise ..... Study ....

My Today's Schedule :

2 am
----
3 am
----
4 am
----
5 am
----
6 am
----
7 am
----
8 am
----
9 am
----
10 am
----
11 am
----
12 noon
----
1 pm
----
2 pm
----
3 pm
----
4 pm
----
5 pm
----
6 pm
----
7 pm
----
8 pm
----
9 pm
----
10 pm
----
11 pm
----
12 midnight
----
1 am

My Weight Today : ....

Rate Today's Efforts Out of 10 for & Sign

FASTED

19 Ramadan

Juz' 19 : Al-Furqān (25:21) - An-Naml (27:55)

My Quran Today

	Surah / Ayah	From	To
Arabic Reading	....	....	....
Translation	....	....	....
Memorising	....	....	....
Tafseer	....	....	....

Scan For Today's Quran

My Prayers Today ☑

- Maghrib
- Isha
- Taraweeh
- Tahajjud
- Fajr
- Zuhr
- Asr

My Dhikr Today

- First Kalima e Tayyab ....
- Astaghfaar & Towbah ....
- Alhamdulillah ....
- ....
- ....
- ....
- ....

My Charity Today

- Zakaat ....
- Sadqa ....
- Khairaat ....
- Fitr ....
- Feed Hungry Person ....
- Help Needy Person ....
- ....

My One Bad Habit To Remove Today

Bad Habit : ....
....

Action To Remove It : ....
....
....
....

My Meals Planner

Suhoor : Dates, Water, Honey,
Habbatussauda (Kalonji) ....
....
Iftar : Dates, Water, ...
....
....

Scan For Today's Lecture

Success
Strategy

PLAN Tomorrow	....
TRACK Today	✓

To be a Better Person, Today, I,

Said **SORRY** to, ..., for ....

Said **THANK YOU** to, ..., for ....

Have **FORGIVEN** to, ..., & I am feeling ....

Phoned / Talked to my **Family Member / Relative / Friend / Neighbour**, ...

Thank Allah for,	**Ask Forgiveness from Allah for,**	**Make Dua to Allah for,**
Water, you Drink	Wasting Water	People, who don't have Water

English Date : ....

Day : ....

⦿ Any Out Of Town Travel Plan Today : ....

Today's Work Priorities :

⦿ 1..
⦿ 2..
⦿ 3..
⦿ 4..
⦿ 5..

Today's Important Meetings / Calls / Visits :

⦿ 1..
⦿ 2..
⦿ 3..
⦿ 4..
⦿ 5..

Today's Financial / Bills / Payment Priorities :

⦿ 1..
⦿ 2..
⦿ 3..
⦿ 4..
⦿ 5..

Today's Family Priorities :

⦿ 1..
⦿ 2..
⦿ 3..

Today's Shopping List :

⦿ ....   ⦿ ....
⦿ ....   ⦿ ....
⦿ ....   ⦿ ....
⦿ ....   ⦿ ....

My Time Planning Today (in Hours / Minutes)

⦿ Sleep .... ⦿ Work .... ⦿ Ibadaah ....

⦿ Family .... ⦿ Exercise ..... ⦿ Study ....

My Today's Schedule :

2 am
----
3 am
----
4 am
----
5 am
----
6 am
----
7 am
----
8 am
----
9 am
----
10 am
----
11 am
----
12 noon
----
1 pm
----
2 pm
----
3 pm
----
4 pm
----
5 pm
----
6 pm
----
7 pm
----
8 pm
----
9 pm
----
10 pm
----
11 pm
----
12 midnight
----
1 am

⦿ **My Weight Today** : ....

Rate Today's Efforts Out of 10 for & Sign

FASTED

20 Ramadan

Juz' 20 : An-Naml (27:56) - Al-'Ankabūt (29:45)

My Quran Today

	Surah / Ayah	From	To
Arabic Reading	....	....	....
Translation	....	....	....
Memorising	....	....	....
Tafseer	....	....	....

Scan For Today's Quran

My Prayers Today ☑

- Maghrib
- Isha
- Taraweeh
- Tahajjud
- Fajr
- Zuhr
- Asr

My Dhikr Today

- First Kalima e Tayyab ....
- Astaghfaar & Towbah ....
- Alhamdulillah ....
- ....
- ....
- ....
- ....

My Charity Today

- Zakaat ....
- Sadqa ....
- Khairaat ....
- Fitr ....
- Feed Hungry Person ....
- Help Needy Person ....
- ....

My One Bad Habit To Remove Today

Bad Habit : ....

....

Action To Remove It : ....

....

....

....

My Meals Planner

Suhoor : Dates, Water, Honey,

Habbatussauda (Kalonji) ....

....

Iftar : Dates, Water, ...

....

....

Scan For Today's Lecture

Success
Strategy

PLAN .... Tomorrow
TRACK Today ✓

To be a Better Person, Today, I,

Said **SORRY** to, ..., for ....

Said **THANK YOU** to, ..., for ....

Have **FORGIVEN** to, ..., & I am feeling ....

Phoned / Talked to my **Family Member / Relative / Friend / Neighbour**, ...

Thank Allah for,	Ask Forgiveness from Allah for,	Make Dua to Allah for,
the Cloths you wear	Arrogance	People, who don't have Cloths

English Date : ....

Day : ....

Any Out Of Town Travel Plan Today : ....

Today's Work Priorities :

1..
2..
3..
4..
5..

Today's Important Meetings / Calls / Visits :

1..
2..
3..
4..
5..

Today's Financial / Bills / Payment Priorities :

1..
2..
3..
4..
5..

Today's Family Priorities :

1..
2..
3..

Today's Shopping List :

....
....
....
....

My Time Planning Today (in Hours / Minutes)

Sleep .... Work .... Ibadaah ....

Family .... Exercise ..... Study ....

My Today's Schedule :

2 am
----
3 am
----
4 am
----
5 am
----
6 am
----
7 am
----
8 am
----
9 am
----
10 am
----
11 am
----
12 noon
----
1 pm
----
2 pm
----
3 pm
----
4 pm
----
5 pm
----
6 pm
----
7 pm
----
8 pm
----
9 pm
----
10 pm
----
11 pm
----
12 midnight
----
1 am

My Weight Today : ....

Rate Today's Efforts Out of 10 for & Sign

FASTED

21 Ramadan

Juz' 21 : Al-'Ankabūt (29:46) - Al-Aḥzāb (33:30)

My Quran Today

	Surah / Ayah	From	To
Arabic Reading	....	....	....
Translation	....	....	....
Memorising	....	....	....
Tafseer	....	....	....

Scan For Today's Quran

My Prayers Today ☑

- Maghrib
- Isha
- Taraweeh
- Tahajjud
- Fajr
- Zuhr
- Asr

My Dhikr Today

- First Kalima e Tayyab ....
- Astaghfaar & Towbah ....
- Alhamdulillah ....
- ....
- ....
- ....
- ....

My Charity Today

- Zakaat ....
- Sadqa ....
- Khairaat ....
- Fitr ....
- Feed Hungry Person ....
- Help Needy Person ....
- ....

My One Bad Habit To Remove Today

- Bad Habit : ....
  ....
- Action To Remove It : ....
  ....
  ....
  ....

My Meals Planner

- Suhoor : Dates, Water, Honey,
  Habbatussauda (Kalonji) ....
  ....
- Iftar : Dates, Water, ...
  ....
  ....

Scan For Today's Lecture

Success Strategy

PLAN Tomorrow	....
TRACK Today	✓

To be a Better Person, Today, I,

- Said **SORRY** to, ..., for ....
- Said **THANK YOU** to, ..., for ....
- Have **FORGIVEN** to, ..., & I am feeling ....
- Phoned / Talked to my **Family Member / Relative / Friend / Neighbour**, ...

Thank Allah for,	Ask Forgiveness from Allah for,	Make Dua to Allah for,
whatever Peace in your Life	your Anger & Mis-Behaves with others	Peace of Mind

English Date : ....

Day : ....

🌸 Any Out Of Town Travel Plan Today : ....

Today's Work Priorities :

🌸 1..

🌸 2..

🌸 3..

🌸 4..

🌸 5..

Today's Important Meetings / Calls / Visits :

🌸 1..

🌸 2..

🌸 3..

🌸 4..

🌸 5..

Today's Financial / Bills / Payment Priorities :

🌸 1..

🌸 2..

🌸 3..

🌸 4..

🌸 5..

Today's Family Priorities :

🌸 1..

🌸 2..

🌸 3..

Today's Shopping List :

🌸 ....   🌸 ....

🌸 ....   🌸 ....

🌸 ....   🌸 ....

🌸 ....   🌸 ....

My Time Planning Today (in Hours / Minutes)

🌸 Sleep .... 🌸 Work .... 🌸 Ibadaah ....

🌸 Family .... 🌸 Exercise ..... 🌸 Study ....

My Today's Schedule :

2 am
----
3 am
----
4 am
----
5 am
----
6 am
----
7 am
----
8 am
----
9 am
----
10 am
----
11 am
----
12 noon
----
1 pm
----
2 pm
----
3 pm
----
4 pm
----
5 pm
----
6 pm
----
7 pm
----
8 pm
----
9 pm
----
10 pm
----
11 pm
----
12 midnight
----
1 am

🌸 **My Weight Today :** ....

Rate Today's Efforts Out of 10 for & Sign

FASTED

22 Ramadan

Juz' 22 : Al-Aḥzāb (33:31) - Yā Sīn (36:27)

My Quran Today

	Surah / Ayah	From	To
Arabic Reading	....	....	....
Translation	....	....	....
Memorising	....	....	....
Tafseer	....	....	....

Scan For Today's Quran

My Prayers Today ☑

- Maghrib
- Isha
- Taraweeh
- Tahajjud
- Fajr
- Zuhr
- Asr

My Dhikr Today

- First Kalima e Tayyab ....
- Astaghfaar & Towbah ....
- Alhamdulillah ....
- ....
- ....
- ....
- ....

My Charity Today

- Zakaat ....
- Sadqa ....
- Khairaat ....
- Fitr ....
- Feed Hungry Person ....
- Help Needy Person ....
- ....

My One Bad Habit To Remove Today

Bad Habit : ....

....

Action To Remove It : ....

....

....

....

My Meals Planner

Suhoor : Dates, Water, Honey,

Habbatussauda (Kalonji) ....

....

Iftar : Dates, Water, ...

....

....

Scan For Today's Lecture

Success   PLAN ....
Strategy Tomorrow
            TRACK ✓
            Today

To be a Better Person, Today, I,

- Said **SORRY** to, ..., for ....
- Said **THANK YOU** to, ..., for ....
- Have **FORGIVEN** to, ..., & I am feeling ....
- Phoned / Talked to my **Family Member / Relative / Friend / Neighbour**, ...

Thank Allah for,	Ask Forgiveness from Allah for,	Make Dua to Allah for,
your Work / Job / Business	missed Salats due to your Work (if any)	People, who don't have Jobs

English Date : ....

Day : ....

⊙ Any Out Of Town Travel Plan Today : ....

Today's Work Priorities :

⊙ 1..

⊙ 2..

⊙ 3..

⊙ 4..

⊙ 5..

Today's Important Meetings / Calls / Visits :

⊙ 1..

⊙ 2..

⊙ 3..

⊙ 4..

⊙ 5..

Today's Financial / Bills / Payment Priorities :

⊙ 1..

⊙ 2..

⊙ 3..

⊙ 4..

⊙ 5..

Today's Family Priorities :

⊙ 1..

⊙ 2..

⊙ 3..

Today's Shopping List :

⊙ ....   ⊙ ....

⊙ ....   ⊙ ....

⊙ ....   ⊙ ....

⊙ ....   ⊙ ....

My Time Planning Today (in Hours / Minutes)

⊙ Sleep .... ⊙ Work .... ⊙ Ibadaah ....

⊙ Family .... ⊙ Exercise ..... ⊙ Study ....

My Today's Schedule :

2 am
_____
3 am
_____
4 am
_____
5 am
_____
6 am
_____
7 am
_____
8 am
_____
9 am
_____
10 am
_____
11 am
_____
12 noon
_____
1 pm
_____
2 pm
_____
3 pm
_____
4 pm
_____
5 pm
_____
6 pm
_____
7 pm
_____
8 pm
_____
9 pm
_____
10 pm
_____
11 pm
_____
12 midnight
_____
1 am
_____

⊙ **My Weight Today :** ....

Rate Today's Efforts Out of 10 for & Sign

FASTED

23 Ramadan

Juz' 23 : Yā Sīn (36:28) - Az-Zumar (39:31)

A Name of My Allah

AR-RAAFI'

The Exalter, The Elevator

My Quran Today

	Surah / Ayah	From	To
Arabic Reading	....	....	....
Translation	....	....	....
Memorising	....	....	....
Tafseer	....	....	....

Scan For Today's Quran

My Prayers Today ☑

- Maghrib
- Isha
- Taraweeh
- Tahajjud
- Fajr
- Zuhr
- Asr

My Dhikr Today

First Kalima e Tayyab ....

Astaghfaar & Towbah ....

Alhamdulillah ....

....

....

....

....

My Charity Today

Zakaat ....

Sadqa ....

Khairaat ....

Fitr ....

Feed Hungry Person ....

Help Needy Person ....

....

My One Bad Habit To Remove Today

Bad Habit : ....

....

Action To Remove It : ....

..............,......................................

....

....

My Meals Planner

Suhoor : Dates, Water, Honey,

Habbatussauda (Kalonji) ....

....

Iftar : Dates, Water, ...

....

....

....

Scan For Today's Lecture

Success Strategy

PLAN .... Tomorrow
TRACK Today ✓

To be a Better Person, Today, I,

Said **SORRY** to, ..., for ....

Said **THANK YOU** to, ..., for ....

Have **FORGIVEN** to, ..., & I am feeling ....

Phoned / Talked to my **Family Member / Relative / Friend / Neighbour**, ...

Thank Allah for,	Ask Forgiveness from Allah for,	Make Dua to Allah for,
Free Air you Breath in	Polluting Allah's Nature	Protection from Natural Disaster

English Date : ....

Day : ....

○ Any Out Of Town Travel Plan Today : ....

Today's Work Priorities :

○ 1..

○ 2..

○ 3..

○ 4..

○ 5..

Today's Important Meetings / Calls / Visits :

○ 1..

○ 2..

○ 3..

○ 4..

○ 5..

Today's Financial / Bills / Payment Priorities :

○ 1..

○ 2..

○ 3..

○ 4..

○ 5..

Today's Family Priorities :

○ 1..

○ 2..

○ 3..

Today's Shopping List :

○ ....   ○ ....

○ ....   ○ ....

○ ....   ○ ....

○ ....   ○ ....

My Time Planning Today (in Hours / Minutes)

○ Sleep .... ○ Work .... ○ Ibadaah ....

○ Family .... ○ Exercise ..... ○ Study ....

My Today's Schedule :

2 am
----
3 am
----
4 am
----
5 am
----
6 am
----
7 am
----
8 am
----
9 am
----
10 am
----
11 am
----
12 noon
----
1 pm
----
2 pm
----
3 pm
----
4 pm
----
5 pm
----
6 pm
----
7 pm
----
8 pm
----
9 pm
----
10 pm
----
11 pm
----
12 midnight
----
1 am

○ **My Weight Today** : ....

Rate Today's Efforts Out of 10 for & Sign

FASTED

24 Ramadan

Juz' 24 : Az-Zumar (39:32) - Fuṣṣilat (41:46)

My Quran Today

	Surah / Ayah	From	To
Arabic Reading	....	....	....
Translation	....	....	....
Memorising	....	....	....
Tafseer	....	....	....

Scan For Today's Quran

My Prayers Today ☑

- Maghrib
- Isha
- Taraweeh
- Tahajjud
- Fajr
- Zuhr
- Asr

My Dhikr Today

- First Kalima e Tayyab ....
- Astaghfaar & Towbah ....
- Alhamdulillah ....
- ....
- ....
- ....
- ....

My Charity Today

- Zakaat ....
- Sadqa ....
- Khairaat ....
- Fitr ....
- Feed Hungry Person ....
- Help Needy Person ....
- ....

My One Bad Habit To Remove Today

Bad Habit : ....

....

Action To Remove It : ....

....

....

....

My Meals Planner

Suhoor : Dates, Water, Honey,

Habbatussauda (Kalonji) ....

....

Iftar : Dates, Water, ...

....

....

Scan For Today's Lecture

Success *Strategy*

PLAN .... Tomorrow
TRACK ✓ Today

To be a Better Person, Today, I,

Said **SORRY** to, ..., for ....

Said **THANK YOU** to, ..., for ....

Have **FORGIVEN** to, ..., & I am feeling ....

Phoned / Talked to my **Family Member / Relative / Friend / Neighbour**, ...

Thank Allah for,	Ask Forgiveness from Allah for,	Make Dua to Allah for,
Quran	not Reading & Following Quran, to the fullest	making you a Better Muslim

English Date : ....

Day : ....

○ Any Out Of Town Travel Plan Today : ....

Today's Work Priorities :

✦ 1...

✦ 2...

○ 3...

○ 4...

○ 5...

Today's Important Meetings / Calls / Visits :

○ 1...

○ 2...

○ 3...

○ 4...

○ 5...

Today's Financial / Bills / Payment Priorities :

○ 1...

○ 2...

○ 3...

○ 4...

○ 5...

Today's Family Priorities :

○ 1...

○ 2...

○ 3...

Today's Shopping List :

○ ....   ○ ....

○ ....   ○ ....

○ ....   ○ ....

○ ....   ○ ....

My Time Planning Today (in Hours / Minutes)

○ Sleep .... ○ Work .... ○ Ibadaah ....

○ Family .... ○ Exercise ..... ○ Study ....

My Today's Schedule :

2 am
----
3 am
----
4 am
----
5 am
----
6 am
----
7 am
----
8 am
----
9 am
----
10 am
----
11 am
----
12 noon
----
1 pm
----
2 pm
----
3 pm
----
4 pm
----
5 pm
----
6 pm
----
7 pm
----
8 pm
----
9 pm
----
10 pm
----
11 pm
----
12 midnight
----
1 am

○ **My Weight Today :** ....

Rate Today's Efforts Out of 10 for & Sign

www.DeeneeShop.com

FASTED

25 Ramadan

Juz' 25 : Fuṣṣilat (41:47) - Al-Jāthiyah (45:37)

My Quran Today

	Surah / Ayah	From	To
Arabic Reading	....	....	....
Translation	....	....	....
Memorising	....	....	....
Tafseer	....	....	....

Scan For Today's Quran

My Prayers Today ☑

- Maghrib
- Isha
- Taraweeh
- Tahajjud
- Fajr
- Zuhr
- Asr

My Dhikr Today

- First Kalima e Tayyab ....
- Astaghfaar & Towbah ....
- Alhamdulillah ....
- ....
- ....
- ....
- ....

My Charity Today

- Zakaat ....
- Sadqa ....
- Khairaat ....
- Fitr ....
- Feed Hungry Person ....
- Help Needy Person ....
- ....

My One Bad Habit To Remove Today

Bad Habit : ....

....

Action To Remove It : ....

....

....

....

My Meals Planner

Suhoor : Dates, Water, Honey,

Habbatussauda (Kalonji) ....

....

Iftar : Dates, Water, ...

....

....

Scan For Today's Lecture

Success Strategy

PLAN .... Tomorrow
TRACK Today ✓

To be a Better Person, Today, I,

Said **SORRY** to, ..., for ....

Said **THANK YOU** to, ..., for ....

Have **FORGIVEN** to, ..., & I am feeling ....

Phoned / Talked to my **Family Member / Relative / Friend / Neighbour**, ...

Thank Allah for,	Ask Forgiveness from Allah for,	Make Dua to Allah to,
your Neighbourhood	not Caring your Neighbours, to the best	give you Good Neighbours

English Date : ....

Day : ....

🌙 Any Out Of Town Travel Plan Today : ....

Today's Work Priorities :

🌙 1..

🌙 2..

🌙 3..

🌙 4..

🌙 5..

Today's Important Meetings / Calls / Visits :

🌙 1..

🌙 2..

🌙 3..

🌙 4..

🌙 5..

Today's Financial / Bills / Payment Priorities :

🌙 1..

🌙 2..

🌙 3..

🌙 4..

🌙 5..

Today's Family Priorities :

🌙 1..

🌙 2..

🌙 3..

Today's Shopping List :

🌙 ....   🌙 ....

🌙 ....   🌙 ....

🌙 ....   🌙 ....

🌙 ....   🌙 ....

My Time Planning Today (in Hours / Minutes)

🌙 Sleep .... 🌙 Work .... 🌙 Ibadaah ....

🌙 Family .... 🌙 Exercise ..... 🌙 Study ....

My Today's Schedule :

2 am
----
3 am
----
4 am
----
5 am
----
6 am
----
7 am
----
8 am
----
9 am
----
10 am
----
11 am
----
12 noon
----
1 pm
----
2 pm
----
3 pm
----
4 pm
----
5 pm
----
6 pm
----
7 pm
----
8 pm
----
9 pm
----
10 pm
----
11 pm
----
12 midnight
----
1 am

🌙 **My Weight Today :** ....

Rate Today's Efforts Out of 10 for & Sign

FASTED

26 Ramadan

Juz' 26 : Al-Aḥqāf (46:1) - Adh-Dhāriyāt (51:30)

My Quran Today

	Surah / Ayah	From	To
Arabic Reading	....	....	....
Translation	....	....	....
Memorising	....	....	....
Tafseer	....	....	....

Scan For Today's Quran

My Prayers Today ☑

- Maghrib
- Isha
- Taraweeh
- Tahajjud
- Fajr
- Zuhr
- Asr

My Dhikr Today

- First Kalima e Tayyab ....
- Astaghfaar & Towbah ....
- Alhamdulillah ....
- ....
- ....
- ....
- ....

My Charity Today

- Zakaat ....
- Sadqa ....
- Khairaat ....
- Fitr ....
- Feed Hungry Person ....
- Help Needy Person ....
- ....

My One Bad Habit To Remove Today

Bad Habit : ....

....

Action To Remove It : ....

....

....

....

My Meals Planner

Suhoor : Dates, Water, Honey,

Habbatussauda (Kalonji) ....

....

Iftar : Dates, Water, ...

....

....

Scan For Today's Lecture

Success Strategy

PLAN .... Tomorrow
TRACK Today ✓

To be a Better Person, Today, I,

Said **SORRY** to, ..., for ....

Said **THANK YOU** to, ..., for ....

Have **FORGIVEN** to, ..., & I am feeling ....

Phoned / Talked to my **Family Member / Relative / Friend / Neighbour**, ...

Thank Allah for,	Ask Forgiveness from Allah for,	Make Dua to Allah for,
his Patience, against your Sins	All your Small & Big Sins	Purification of your Heart

English Date : ....

Day : ....

Any Out Of Town Travel Plan Today : ....

Today's Work Priorities :

1..
2..
3..
4..
5..

Today's Important Meetings / Calls / Visits :

1..
2..
3..
4..
5..

Today's Financial / Bills / Payment Priorities :

1..
2..
3..
4..
5..

Today's Family Priorities :

1..
2..
3..

Today's Shopping List :

....
....
....
....

My Time Planning Today (in Hours / Minutes)

Sleep .... Work .... Ibadaah ....

Family .... Exercise ..... Study ....

My Today's Schedule :

2 am
----
3 am
----
4 am
----
5 am
----
6 am
----
7 am
----
8 am
----
9 am
----
10 am
----
11 am
----
12 noon
----
1 pm
----
2 pm
----
3 pm
----
4 pm
----
5 pm
----
6 pm
----
7 pm
----
8 pm
----
9 pm
----
10 pm
----
11 pm
----
12 midnight
----
1 am

My Weight Today : ....

Rate Today's Efforts Out of 10 for & Sign

FASTED

27 Ramadan

Juz' 27 : Adh-Dhāriyāt (51:31) - Al-Ḥadīd (57:29)

My Quran Today

	Surah / Ayah	From	To
Arabic Reading	....	....	....
Translation	....	....	....
Memorising	....	....	....
Tafseer	....	....	....

Scan For Today's Quran

My Prayers Today ☑

- Maghrib
- Isha
- Taraweeh
- Tahajjud
- Fajr
- Zuhr
- Asr

My Dhikr Today

- First Kalima e Tayyab ....
- Astaghfaar & Towbah ....
- Alhamdulillah ....
- ....
- ....
- ....
- ....

My Charity Today

- Zakaat ....
- Sadqa ....
- Khairaat ....
- Fitr ....
- Feed Hungry Person ....
- Help Needy Person ....
- ....

My One Bad Habit To Remove Today

Bad Habit : ....
....

Action To Remove It : ....
....
....
....

My Meals Planner

Suhoor : Dates, Water, Honey,
Habbatussauda (Kalonji) ....
....
Iftar : Dates, Water, ...
....
....

Scan For Today's Lecture

Success
Strategy

PLAN .... Tomorrow
TRACK Today ✓

To be a Better Person, Today, I,

Said **SORRY** to, ..., for ....

Said **THANK YOU** to, ..., for ....

Have **FORGIVEN** to, ..., & I am feeling ....

Phoned / Talked to my **Family Member / Relative / Friend / Neighbour**, ...

Thank Allah for,	Ask Forgiveness from Allah for,	Make Dua to Allah for,
creating Laylatul-Qadr	All of your Sins, done Publically or Privately	getting the Laylatul-Qadr

English Date : ....

Day : ....

Any Out Of Town Travel Plan Today : ....

Today's Work Priorities :

1..
2..
3..
4..
5..

Today's Important Meetings / Calls / Visits :

1..
2..
3..
4..
5..

Today's Financial / Bills / Payment Priorities :

1..
2..
3..
4..
5..

Today's Family Priorities :

1..
2..
3..

Today's Shopping List :

....
....
....
....

My Time Planning Today (in Hours / Minutes)

Sleep ....   Work ....   Ibadaah ....

Family ....   Exercise .....   Study ....

My Today's Schedule :

2 am
----
3 am
----
4 am
----
5 am
----
6 am
----
7 am
----
8 am
----
9 am
----
10 am
----
11 am
----
12 noon
----
1 pm
----
2 pm
----
3 pm
----
4 pm
----
5 pm
----
6 pm
----
7 pm
----
8 pm
----
9 pm
----
10 pm
----
11 pm
----
12 midnight
----
1 am

My Weight Today : ....

Rate Today's Efforts Out of 10 for & Sign

FASTED

28 Ramadan

Juz' 28 : Al-Mujādilah (58:1) - At-Taḥrīm (66:12)

My Quran Today

	Surah / Ayah	From	To
Arabic Reading	....	....	....
Translation	....	....	....
Memorising	....	....	....
Tafseer	....	....	....

Scan For Today's Quran

My Prayers Today ☑

- Maghrib
- Isha
- Taraweeh
- Tahajjud
- Fajr
- Zuhr
- Asr

My Dhikr Today

- First Kalima e Tayyab ....
- Astaghfaar & Towbah ....
- Alhamdulillah ....
- ....
- ....
- ....
- ....

My Charity Today

- Zakaat ....
- Sadqa ....
- Khairaat ....
- Fitr ....
- Feed Hungry Person ....
- Help Needy Person ....
- ....

My One Bad Habit To Remove Today

- Bad Habit : ....
  ....
- Action To Remove It : ....
  ....
  ....
  ....

My Meals Planner

- Suhoor : Dates, Water, Honey, Habbatussauda (Kalonji) ....
  ....
- Iftar : Dates, Water, ...
  ....
  ....

Scan For Today's Lecture

Success Strategy

PLAN	
Tomorrow	
TRACK	✓
Today	

To be a Better Person, Today, I,

- Said **SORRY** to, ..., for ....
- Said **THANK YOU** to, ..., for ....
- Have **FORGIVEN** to, ..., & I am feeling ....
- Phoned / Talked to my **Family Member / Relative / Friend / Neighbour**, ...

Thank Allah for,	Ask Forgiveness from Allah for,	Make Dua to Allah for,
the Friends you have	not Benefitting your Friends, to the fullest	Righteous Good Friends

English Date : ....

Day : ....

○ Any Out Of Town Travel Plan Today : ....

Today's Work Priorities :

○ 1...

○ 2...

○ 3...

○ 4...

○ 5...

Today's Important Meetings / Calls / Visits :

○ 1...

○ 2...

○ 3...

○ 4...

○ 5...

Today's Financial / Bills / Payment Priorities :

○ 1...

○ 2...

○ 3...

○ 4...

○ 5...

Today's Family Priorities :

○ 1...

○ 2...

○ 3...

Today's Shopping List :

○ ....   ○ ....

○ ....   ○ ....

○ ....   ○ ....

○ ....   ○ ....

My Time Planning Today (in Hours / Minutes)

○ Sleep .... ○ Work .... ○ Ibadaah ....

○ Family .... ○ Exercise ..... ○ Study ....

My Today's Schedule :

2 am

3 am

4 am

5 am

6 am

7 am

8 am

9 am

10 am

11 am

12 noon

1 pm

2 pm

3 pm

4 pm

5 pm

6 pm

7 pm

8 pm

9 pm

10 pm

11 pm

12 midnight

1 am

○ **My Weight Today** : ....

Rate Today's Efforts Out of 10 for & Sign

29 Ramadan

Juz' 29 : Al-Mulk (67:1) - Al-Mursalāt (77:50)

My Quran Today

	Surah / Ayah	From	To
Arabic Reading	....	....	....
Translation	....	....	....
Memorising	....	....	....
Tafseer	....	....	....

Scan For Today's Quran

My Prayers Today ☑

- Maghrib
- Isha
- Taraweeh
- Tahajjud
- Fajr
- Zuhr
- Asr

My Dhikr Today

- First Kalima e Tayyab ....
- Astaghfaar & Towbah ....
- Alhamdulillah ....
- ....
- ....
- ....
- ....

My Charity Today

- Zakaat ....
- Sadqa ....
- Khairaat ....
- Fitr ....
- Feed Hungry Person ....
- Help Needy Person ....
- ....

My One Bad Habit To Remove Today

Bad Habit : ....
....
Action To Remove It : ....
....
....
....

My Meals Planner

Suhoor : Dates, Water, Honey, Habbatussauda (Kalonji) ....
....
Iftar : Dates, Water, ...
....
....

Scan For Today's Lecture

Success Strategy

PLAN Tomorrow	....
TRACK Today	✓

To be a Better Person, Today, I,

- Said **SORRY** to, ..., for ....
- Said **THANK YOU** to, ..., for ....
- Have **FORGIVEN** to, ..., & I am feeling ....
- Phoned / Talked to my **Family Member / Relative / Friend / Neighbour**, ...

Thank Allah for,	Ask Forgiveness from Allah for,	Make Dua to Allah for,
You being Alive	Shirk (believing other than Allah) (if any)	Jannah (Paradise)

FASTED

English Date : ....

Day : ....

⬤ Any Out Of Town Travel Plan Today : ....

Today's Work Priorities :

⬤ 1..

⬤ 2..

⬤ 3..

⬤ 4..

⬤ 5..

Today's Important Meetings / Calls / Visits :

⬤ 1..

⬤ 2..

⬤ 3..

⬤ 4..

⬤ 5..

Today's Financial / Bills / Payment Priorities :

⬤ 1..

⬤ 2..

⬤ 3..

⬤ 4..

⬤ 5..

Today's Family Priorities :

⬤ 1..

⬤ 2..

⬤ 3..

Today's Shopping List :

⬤ ....   ⬤ ....

⬤ ....   ⬤ ....

⬤ ....   ⬤ ....

⬤ ....   ⬤ ....

My Time Planning Today (in Hours / Minutes)

⬤ Sleep .... ⬤ Work .... ⬤ Ibadaah ....

⬤ Family .... ⬤ Exercise ..... ⬤ Study ....

My Today's Schedule :

2 am
----
3 am
----
4 am
----
5 am
----
6 am
----
7 am
----
8 am
----
9 am
----
10 am
----
11 am
----
12 noon
----
1 pm
----
2 pm
----
3 pm
----
4 pm
----
5 pm
----
6 pm
----
7 pm
----
8 pm
----
9 pm
----
10 pm
----
11 pm
----
12 midnight
----
1 am

⬤ **My Weight Today** : ....

Rate Today's Efforts Out of 10 for & Sign

FASTED

30 Ramadan

Juz' 30 : An-Naba' (78:1) - An-Nās (114:6)

My Quran Today

	Surah / Ayah	From	To
Arabic Reading	....	....	....
Translation	....	....	....
Memorising	....	....	....
Tafseer	....	....	....

Scan For Today's Quran

My Prayers Today ☑

- Maghrib
- Isha
- Taraweeh
- Tahajjud
- Fajr
- Zuhr
- Asr

My Dhikr Today

- First Kalima e Tayyab ....
- Astaghfaar & Towbah ....
- Alhamdulillah ....
- ....
- ....
- ....
- ....

My Charity Today

- Zakaat ....
- Sadqa ....
- Khairaat ....
- Fitr ....
- Feed Hungry Person ....
- Help Needy Person ....
- ....

My One Bad Habit To Remove Today

- Bad Habit : ....
  ....
- Action To Remove It : ....
  ....
  ....
  ....

My Meals Planner

- Suhoor : Dates, Water, Honey,
  Habbatussauda (Kalonji) ....
  ....
- Iftar : Dates, Water, ...
  ....
  ....

Scan For Today's Lecture

Success | PLAN .... Tomorrow
Strategy | TRACK Today ✓

To be a Better Person, Today, I,

- Said **SORRY** to, ..., for ....
- Said **THANK YOU** to, ..., for ....
- Have **FORGIVEN** to, ..., & I am feeling ....
- Phoned / Talked to my **Family Member / Relative / Friend / Neighbour**, ...

Thank Allah for,	Ask Forgiveness from Allah for,	Make Dua to Allah for,
Eid-Ul-Fitr	all Missed Ibaadah in this Ramadan	Entire Muslim Ummah

English Date : ....

Day : ....

⚬ Any Out Of Town Travel Plan Today : ....

Today's Work Priorities :

⚬ 1..

⚬ 2..

⚬ 3..

⚬ 4..

⚬ 5..

Today's Important Meetings / Calls / Visits :

⚬ 1..

⚬ 2..

⚬ 3..

⚬ 4..

⚬ 5..

Today's Financial / Bills / Payment Priorities :

⚬ 1..

⚬ 2..

⚬ 3..

⚬ 4..

⚬ 5..

Today's Family Priorities :

⚬ 1..

⚬ 2..

⚬ 3..

Today's Shopping List :

⚬ ....   ⚬ ....

⚬ ....   ⚬ ....

⚬ ....   ⚬ ....

⚬ ....   ⚬ ....

My Time Planning Today (in Hours / Minutes)

⚬ Sleep .... ⚬ Work .... ⚬ Ibadaah ....

⚬ Family .... ⚬ Exercise ..... ⚬ Study ....

My Today's Schedule :

2 am
----
3 am
----
4 am
----
5 am
----
6 am
----
7 am
----
8 am
----
9 am
----
10 am
----
11 am
----
12 noon
----
1 pm
----
2 pm
----
3 pm
----
4 pm
----
5 pm
----
6 pm
----
7 pm
----
8 pm
----
9 pm
----
10 pm
----
11 pm
----
12 midnight
----
1 am

⚬ **My Weight Today** : ....

Rate Today's Efforts Out of 10 for & Sign

ZAKAT

What is Zakat?

Zakat or Zakah is one of the five pillars of Islam, that Allah imposed on the <u>Rich Muslims</u>, an obligatory annual payment; It is deducted for the poor, so it would be one of the ways of ending misery, spreading happiness, and relieving the needy from the troubles of life. As for Zakat ruling, it is an obligation in Islam. Allah the Almighty says: "<u>establish prayer and give Zakah</u>". It is also established in the Sunnah of the Prophet, peace be upon him.

What is Nisab?

Nisab is the threshold for which a Muslim's personal wealth must be above if he or she is to be eligible to pay Zakat., If the money reaches the Nisab, a lunar year has passed on it and its owner has full ownership, the Zakat on the money must be paid by its owner, and its amount is one quarter of a tenth (<u>2.5%</u>). Nisab of Zakat on money is calculated based on one of the two Nisab values from which the threshold is determined: 85 grams of Gold, 595 grams of Silver.

Zakat on Gold or Silver

The gold or silver on which Zakat is due is the gold and silver that is owned for trade or saving, then Zakat must be paid on it if its amount reaches the Nisab of Zakat (85 grams or more on Gold or 595 grams or more on Silver), so the owner must pay a quarter of a tenth (2.5%) of that amount of gold or silver.

Whom can we give zakat to?

The Holy Quran defines eight categories who are entitled to receive Zakat:

- <u>The poor</u>, who do not have sufficient wealth or income to fulfill their needs, such as food, drink, and clothing;
- <u>The needy</u>, who do not afford their essential needs although they may have a source of income;
- <u>Those employed to collect or administer the funds of Zakat</u>; though they are not poor, they may be given some of the Zakat.
- <u>Reconciliation of hearts</u>; These are people who may be given Zakat in order to open their hearts towards Islam.
- <u>Slaves</u>, and they include three groups: a) indentured Muslim servants who have contracts with their owners to be freed upon paying a sum of money, b) slaves who may be bought with Zakat funds and set free, and c) Muslim prisoners.
- <u>The indebted</u>, who are unable to pay off their debts.
- <u>For Allah's Cause</u>, where the Zakat is paid for those fighting in the way of Allah (Jihad), and for other costs of Jihad.
- <u>The wayfarer</u>, they are travelers who are cut off from everything, so they may be given from Zakat to help them reach their homes.

ZAKAT